rhapsody 2020
an anthology of guelph writing

Vocamus Press
Guelph, Ontario

Presented by Vocamus Writers Community

Published by Vocamus Press
© All rights reserved

Edited by Michael Kleiza

Cover image by Tudor Costache
 Some rights reserved

ISBN 13: 978-1-77422-036-8 (pbk)
ISBN 13: 978-1-77422-035-1 (ebk)

Vocamus Press
130 Dublin Street, North
Guelph, Ontario, Canada
N1H 4N4

www.vocamus.net

2020

Preface

The Rhapsody Anthology is an annual collection of Guelph and area poetry presented by Vocamus Writers Community, a non-profit community organization that supports literary culture in Guelph, Ontario.

The anthology is a celebration of local writing that includes both authors who are well established in their craft and those who are published here for the first time, reflecting the writers and writing that formed the literary communities of Guelph during the year 2019/2020.

The collection was edited by Michael Kleiza. The cover art was provided by Tudor Costache. The cover and interior were designed by Jeremy Luke Hill.

Acknowledgments

The Rhapsody Anthology is produced by Vocamus Writers Community, a non-profit community organization that supports writing, publishing, and book culture in the Guelph area.

This year our work has been generously supported by June Blair, Carol Dilworth, Martina Freitag, Paul Hock, Marie-Claire Recurt, Albert Marsolais, Deb Stark, Lauren Stein, and Marian Thorpe. We appreciate their support very much. If you'd also like to support the work of Vocamus Writers Community you can do so by searching us on www.fundrazr.com.

Thanks to Michael Kleiza for editing the collection. Thanks to all the contributors for sharing their work so generously. Thanks to Tudor Costache for allowing his photograph to be used for the book cover. Thanks finally to all those who contribute to the literary culture of Guelph as readers, writers, publishers, sponsors, venues, broadcasters, and in countless other ways – this collection is a celebration of all that you do.

rhapsody 2020
an anthology of guelph writing

Table of Contents

The Unraveling   1
Darcy Hiltz

Charles Watkins   3
Jeremy Luke Hill

Dissolving Hour   5
Jeffrey Reid Pettis

Solstice Swifts   7
Greg Kennedy

Ghost in the House   9
Valerie Senyk

Military Portrait   11
Robert Penfold

Gathering Stones   13
Bieke Stengos

The Oxford Book of Modern Verse   15
Nicholas Ruddock

The People Are Pulling Away   17
Adam Maue

Sticky Faux Leather   19
Alison Thompson

Meditation   21
Michael Kleiza

Mennonite Wife Prayer: Chokecherry   23
Karen Houle

Husband   25
Sandy Bassie

Autotomy   27
Greg Rhyno

10-7   29
Candace De Taeye

Sea Slugs   31
Jerry Prager

Slouching Toward Tomorrow   33
James Clarke

Night Songs   35
Melinda Burns

A Song in That   37
Rob O'Flanagan

afterimage   39
Sheri Doyle

the early bird   41
Sheila Koop

Rejection Letter   43
Tom Vaine

The Unraveling
Darcy Hiltz

Darcy Hiltz is an Archivist / Librarian at Guelph Public Library. A native of Nova Scotia, he holds an MLIS from Dalhousie University and a BA Hons in History and Sociology from Acadia University. He also completed a Certificate in Creative Writing from Conestoga College and a Professional Learning Certificate in Genealogical Studies from the National Institute of Genealogical Studies. In his spare time he writes poetry, is an avid student, tends to his family's history, swims, and assists his father on his farm. He is married and lives in Fergus, Ontario.

The Unraveling

    sweat
    soaks
    pools like rain
    in low
            lying
                        ground
    stains
    dark
    the cotton
    underarm
    whites

    pant leg
    bottoms
    drag
            fray
    expose

    t
     h
    r
     e
    a
    d
    s

t o e s poke
heels wear
worn of
steps

travels
of my
landscape

clothes
for
inner
self

Charles Watkins

Jeremy Luke Hill

Jeremy Luke Hill is the publisher at Gordon Hill Press He is also the Managing Director at Vocamus Writers Community, a non-profit community organization that supports book culture in Guelph.

Charles Watkins

I am he, with foreignness struck,
breathing the insupportable air,
where those fomenting justice
from folds of fire, watch eye to eye
through silky fronds of flame.

I see them as in a mirror,
the glossy side of a toppling wave,
a water-smoothed stone shining
like glass, reflecting flesh-time
in scales of time, wrapping together
Andromeda time, galaxy time,
moon time (oh woe and alas),
anything but Earth time.

Down among the dead,
where sweet sleep has dreams
that daylight never knew,
sweet promising dreams,
marvelling visitors who know
and tell that behind (or before),
that down (or up), is the door out
into the sweet light of day.

– from Doris Lessing's
Briefing for a Descent into Hell

Dissolving Hour

Jeffrey Reid Pettis

Jeffrey Reid Pettis lives and works in Guelph as an educator. He listens to loud music loudly ,and his academic interest in literary depictions of paranoia is a fine line of yarn away from a conspiracy theory wall. He mostly sits around and reads, sometimes writes poems, and even more sometimes publishes them.

Dissolving Hour

as they toss pebbles to the sunset in its dissolving hour,
the arcs of their stones cascade in silhouette,
and are reclaimed by the parking lot pavement.

in the afterglow of summer, the tosspots drunk on autumn
savour the splash of frenetic reds enkindling the halls
of leaves along the highway. unoaked chardonnay on fire.

they drink until the flame fades and veils of frost descend
upon their memories: gossamer draped over failed polaroids,
the undeveloped white of winter, amnesiac.

later they feel the ache of phantom limbs
in the struggle to remember, the loss implied
in cataracts, of what falls out of frame, unfocused.

surely there had been a year, but what had it been for?
the ripple unnoticed by the concrete? the music
of stone trickling on stone? echoes written into scores?

Solstice Swifts

Greg Kennedy

Greg Kennedy SJ is a Jesuit priest residing at the Ignatius Jesuit Centre, where he works primarily as a spiritual director He has published two academic books: The Ontology of Trash: the disposable and its problematic nature *(2007) and La* cuidad penitente /The Penitent City *(2018) written in Spanish; a children's book entitled* Amazing Friendships between Animals and Saints; *and a collection of poetry called* Reupholstered Psalms for the Anthropocene. *Central to his vocation are poetry and the Earth.*

Solstice Swifts

Faithful to name and nature,
The swifts dart and dive,
laughing Furies
in a solstice sky
made wide for a playful evening.
The day's gossip spins in twists
and turns of plot and wing,
at times madly flapping,
at times as straight
as arrows sanely shot.
Suddenly light, brick and darkness
align and home unleashes
its deepest pull. The lonely chimney cries.
They curl midflight and fall
as infants into Mother Spirit's lap,
their laughter louder now
so gently swallowed.

Ghost in the House

Valerie Senyk

Valerie Senyk is a multi-media artist. She received her BFA and MA in Drama from the University of Saskatchewan, Saskatoon, and taught Theatre Arts at universities in Saskatchewan and Ontario for over twenty-three years. She is a playwright, an actor, and a recorded performance poet. She has published a full-length volume of poetry, I Want A Poem.

Ghost in the House

We fetched his body
limp and ailing
from the north

Brought him south
made him a bed
a tiny room

Fed him broth and greens
held him close
whispering gentleness

Caught his tears
on our shoulders
our lives were soaked

From time to time
he made it down the stairs
skinny, silent and white

with fear and sickness
every bone broken
every dream broken

He became the ghost
in the house
haunting our every hour

We installed more lights
signals to the way forward

his voice now tells us
where it hurts

Military Portrait

Robert Penfold

Robert Penfold was born in Watford, England. he holds a B.A. (Hons.) English, University of Windsor, 1965; Secondary Teacher Certificates in English and History, University of Western Ontario, 1966; and an M.A. in Elizabethan Literature, Lakehead University, 1976. He taught high school English, covering all levels and grades, from 1966 to 2003. He currently resides with his wife Joanna in the Village by the Arboretum.

Military Portrait

How can you willingly crawl under
That burlap shroud? The last person
I saw do that was Jenkins. We all agreed
He went immediately to the angels,
His death grimace easily brightening to a rictus grin,
Beatific in our puny, self-serving memories.

As your hand emerges from the shroud
I instinctively duck for cover. Momentary panic
Triggers a flood of memories of the trenches.
But now I realize you're not clutching a grenade
To lob between my clay-clogged feet. It's only
The rubber bulb you squeeze to snap the photo.

So I hold this erect, heroic pose,
Hoping Mum and Dad will read confidence
Where really I feel numb and crumpled
Beneath the skin. I know the eyes have it,
Especially in a portrait, so I'll stare down
The tripod balancing your box camera,
Reminiscent of a Bosch machine gun.

This may be the last glimpse anyone gets
Of my living form. So read here the val-
iance
Of the hardened soldier of the line,
Not yet glazed to the weapon's sharpness,
But velvet around the edges, liquid inside
For fallen comrades and family back home.

Phosphorous explosion. Let me out of here!

Gathering Stones

Bieke Stengos

Bieke Stengos was born in Belgium, came to Canada as a young woman, and has lived here ever since, with time spent in various countries overseas. She has published a chapbook, Aunt Ida, *two collections of poetry,* Abandoned by the Muse *and* Transmigrator.

Gathering Stones

Father instructs us to gather flat stones
that have washed up on the beach.
He wants them for the path
he's putting in the garden, back home.
My brother and I marvel
that home is a place
where things happen, even with us gone.

My aunt says, he'll never use the stones,
and she refuses to bend down
to pick up even one.
We coax her because we can't abide
to see her contradict our father.

When she slips on algae,
we laugh with the adults
and watch her walk away,
      her bare feet slapping wet sand,
      her bum, a wiggle of stains.

The Oxford Book of Modern Verse

Nicholas Ruddock

Nicholas Ruddock is author of The Parabolist *(Doubleday 2010),* How Loveta Got Her Baby *(Breakwater 2014), and* Night Ambulance *(Breakwater 2016).*

The Oxford Book of Modern Verse

At the Abbey Theatre, in 1934, she came to the attention of William Butler Yeats. In this photograph, dark hair frames her face, a moonstone, her creamy pallor typical for Ireland back then, before Ryan Air, before the Costa del Sol burnt winter away. An actress less than half his age, her voice was pitch-perfect for singing the old songs, for the recitation of poetry. He saw her first outside, leaning against a shadowed wall, backlit, a parenthesis. Inside, she sang and recited and he spoke to her, his incompetence with girls and women paring him away, saying, with your permission I could edit your verse. Oh the flattering. She was bare to the world, undisguised by metaphor. Leaning towards her, over a small desk, light flickering, he said, Margot, I find rhythm wanting in your body of work. As if she didn't know it, as if she hadn't intended it, as though she hadn't reached out for the very lack of it. Married, a mother of two, a skewed gyroscope, her chameleon moods. Finally he succumbed to her, a touch on her shoulder, unbuttoning her in Donegal in November, the hotel under direct assault by a north wind that had driven even the sheep indoors. He recovered his potency with her, a Second Coming, and in good faith he included seven of her poems in the Oxford Book of Modern Verse, 1936. Then he went to Spain with his wife to translate the Upanishads, but Margot distracted him still, her pulse beating in his head, her white skin addictive, her body his nightmare, a trainwreck, brakes shot uncertain on the narrow-gauge, drive-wheel spinning, the other passengers already jumped for their lives while he stayed, unbalanced, shovelling coal into her, and the heat of her body burnt holes in his hands and his face and his falling-down underwear and his gabardine trousers which were undone to her as dawn broke to that otherwise empty bedroom, to the soporific breezes of Palma, Majorca. The morning post, her letters on a silver tray unanswered. Then Barcelona, where she cleaved and broke, alone in the Plaça de Colom, her only friends dogs and vagrants and midnight vendors of street food, cobblestones, her own footsteps leading up a staircase to an anonymous roof, to a skylight in a green and rusty metal frame, down through which she fell—not as you or I would fall, thinking oh no oh no—with no thought in her torn-up head at all, down through shards of glass to an earthen floor where three Catalans, surprised, used everything at hand to staunch the blood that flowed from her now-glittering veins: tablecloths, restaurant linen, napkins, aprons stained with the juice of beets and prunes and mustard, the sauce of soups and apples, daubing and pressing until they ran to the street and waved down the Guàrdia Urbana and the Guàrdia Urbana carried her away. Next she entered a series of hospitals from which she never recovered, and in our world today, 2018, no mention is made of her, of Margot Ruddock, nor is she included in The Oxford Book of Modern Verse, but the wild swans at Coole still turn their heads, and falcons twist against leather restraints, and the bishops of Ireland remain as mute as ever to the sounds the wounded make.

The People Are Pulling Away

Adam Maue

Adam Maue moved to Guelph on a whim in 2016. Since then he's worked odd jobs, volunteered, and made friends there during the winter, and he's spent his summers traveling Canada by train. He hopes to keep doing what he's doing until the next adventure comes along.

The People Are Pulling Away

I'm afraid to say
the people are pulling away.

some restless but tired escape
      moves through our doors.

nobody stays for long
      in our embrace
as they leave early
      with a shameful face.

I'm afraid to say
the people are pulling away.

the friends we had
      were not friends at all
but only strangers/

now take one last look
      at the ones we loved the most
they are beyond the rain, they brought
      to our door.

I'm afraid to say
the people are pulling away
      from the love we gave them.

      they are sailing on a harsh sea
that won't allow them one word
of apology
      or regret.

Sticky Faux Leather

Alison Thompson

Alison Thompson is a screenwriter, author, and poet. She is a recent graduate of the University of Guelph where she majored in English and minored in Creative Writing. She hopes to pursue an MFA in Creative Writing in the near future. She is one of the founders of Writers & Co., a small Guelph initiative that brings together young Guelph writers in order to workshop their writing.

Sticky Faux Leather

Heart beats rapid, quick, churning against my cheek.
An eternal attempt to make my body mean something to you.
Kisses like honey dripping down your chin,
lick it up nice and slow, scream in my ear loud as you can
maybe it will make the voices go away.
Twenty and eleven hour-long dreams and you still
will not look me in the eye.
Cracks splinter through my bones
and shatter on the floor.
Tears bloom on my cheeks
you look right at them, shrug three times.
I'm still sitting on the same couch, the one made of sticky faux leather.
I will be sitting there forever.

Meditation

Michael Kleiza

Michael Kleiza is originally from Montreal. His poems have been published in various anthologies and magazines. His poem "Remembrance Song" was chosen as a finalist for the William Collins Canadian Poetry Prize presented by Descant *magazine. He has read his poetry at many venues, including The Fringe of the Eden Mills Writers' Festival, the Hillside Festival and the Art Bar in Toronto. He is an alumnus of the Wired Writing program at the Banff Centre for Creativity in Alberta. His first collection of poetry, A Poet on the Moon (Vocamus Press), was published in 2015.*

Meditation

i walked a dark cathedral
of cedars leeward
from the wind
stillness followed me
sunshine and crystalline snow
sanctified me
the cry of a solitary crow
cracked the icy silence

Mennonite Wife Prayer: Chokecherry

Karen Houle

Karen Houle is associate professor of philosophy at the University of Guelph in Guelph, Canada. She co-edited a book of essays on Hegel and Deleuze with Jim Vernon entitled, Hegel and Deleuze: Together Again for the First Time. *Her monograph,* Responsibility, Complexity, and Abortion Toward a New Image of Ethical Thought, *was released in 2013. She is also the author of three books of poetry:* Ballast, During, *and the Governor General's Award shortlisted collection,* The Grand River Watershed: A Folk Ecology.

Mennonite Wife Prayer: Chokecherry

The pucker, the rusted bucket pings, a ringing
Plucks the ripeness free, the ladder steadied, and then the
    sourest singing.

The hymnal, it's the humming of her Enoch, a bitterness, a
    waxwing.
The milking time each morning, it's rickety limbs, and then
    the rough unstringing.

Dear Lord,

There is some fruit.
Here are my hands.
My hands are touching the fruit,
Making accidental music in the branches.

Forgive me.

* from *The Grand River Watershed: A Folk Ecology* (Gaspereau Press, 2019)

Husband

Sandy Bassie

Sandy Bassie has maintained a love of language and a passion for writing her entire life. She reveals this in her journals, reflections on life, poetry, and some (very) short stories. She has lived in the Guelph area, first in Acton then in Fergus, for the past twenty-eight years.

Husband

I am the one the nurses call
each time he misbehaves.

I take him for a haircut,
when I can, a shave.
He is good only for me, they say.
It mystifies me knowing this
because he was never that way
when we lived together.

Too many days, my certain truth,
I was in it all alone.

Still, he is my husband,
at least he used to be
when there was history
and happy times... before the drink,
before the debt,
before we lost it all.

And though I know
it's common sense to leave
well enough alone
a little something in me still
reaches for the phone.

No longer at his beck and call
but to another's aid
I will be available.

All my debts are paid.

Autotomy

Greg Rhyno

Greg Rhyno's debut novel To Me You Seem Giant *is now available from NeWest Press. His writing has appeared in* Prism International, Hobart, *and* Riddle Fence. *He's a recent graduate of the University of Guelph's Creative Writing MFA program, and he lives with his family in Guelph, Ontario.*

Autotomy

You press down and cut
through a pepper.
Expose seeds you shouldn't eat,
things you take out with the knife,
and a pregnancy—
the smaller pepper hiding inside.

There are others here, too. Grey mushroom and bleak onion.
Ginger appears animal.
Cut off an arm and wait for it to grow back.

On hot metal and oil,
they whisper simultaneously: a desperate crowd noise,
the sound of dirt sliding endlessly from a shovel.

In my kitchen, you scold me.
My knives are too dull.

The white lines are visible
when you angle your wrist
just so. I don't ask.
I see them the way you can see
hot and cold moving in a sunbeam—
the shadow of something transparent.

*(This is how I imagine it:
The light from the bathroom window is whitish and immobile.
Without heat. Your pupils are large. The sink is stopped and
the faucet running. A part of you falls dark, then brightens
into living stained glass.)*

After dinner,
tea hemorrhages in the pot.
Red water curls and reaches for us with its thin fingers.

10-7

Candace De Taeye

Candace de Taeye's poetry has been published in CV2, Carousel, Echolocation, Feathertale.com *and* Joypuke. *Her first chapbook,* Roe, *was published by PS Guelph in 2015. Her debut full-length collection,* Small Planes and the Dead Fathers of Lovers, *was published by Vocamus Press in 2016. She works as a Paramedic in downtown Toronto. She lives in Guelph with her husband, children, two dogs, two cats, four elderly tree-frogs and a very large tortoise.*

10-7

on scene

off air

into the building envelopes

the real doors open Toronto

      the bath houses, after-hours clubs, shelters in church basements, money counting rooms deep beneath Bay St., greased undercarriages of streetcars, locked dementia wings, sally ports and prisons, the Bridal Path, sweatshops, apartments hoarded to the ceiling or ones with children sleeping on nothing at all

rolling up to hide

'oh mei, oh mei, hold me in your arms'

response time

the time measured from the time notice is received to the earlier of the following

any type of defibrillation

take a pulse / anatomical landmark

the xiphoid process

where the ribs come together

heel of hand two fingers above that point stack hands one on top of the other begin compressions

antecubital fossa /needle stick

(g) be free from all communicable diseases

the HIV clinic of the hospital hidden on a middle floor at the end of a hall, at the end of a hall, around a corner.

patient destination and selection procedures: sure
if any part of the hospital bears your name.

what a

Bundle of His

Sea Slugs

Jerry Prager

Jerry Prager is the author of three volumes on the Calabrian mafia of Guelph, Legends of the Morgeti; *and a series on fugitive slaves and how they came to Wellington County. He is also preparing the first six books of a novel series.*

Sea Slugs

One lies before us on the lee shore,
a giant slug washed up on the beach, a brain-sized,
liver-shaped lump, gray and black-veined, glistening dry,
not yet baked, secreting mauve fluid onto Shell Island Shards.

A second swims up with a muscular grace,
angelic from the depths like a manta ray
flying up the rising floor to beach beside the first
as if to share its fate.

With a forked stick I rescue the first and
restore it to the lee waters; it revives.
The second throbs on the beach.
Set again in the current it re-asserts its will
and beaches again. The first is vanishing below.

Rescued a second time, the second seems to realize
its change in fortune; stretching its wings
from its lump of a body it glides off the other way,
refusing to provide me with a symbol of romantic re-union,
ungrateful blob that it is.
Paul and Pat board, he to the tiller,
she to the lanyards.

Shouldering the bow off the beach
I inch the keel out of the sand.

Straining to catch the current,
I draw myself from the chest-high surf,
from just-cleared rudder depths.

My legs and arms and back surge with
uncommon prowess as I draw myself on board,
a hero in my own eyes again,
despite the slug that rises to watch us go,
mocking me with its lumpy realism.

Slouching Toward Tomorrow

James Clarke

James Clarke was born in Peterborough, Ontario and attended McGill University and Osgoode Hall. He practiced law in Cobourg, Ontario before his appointment to the Bench in 1983. Clarke served as a judge of the Superior Court of Ontario and is now retired, residing in Guelph, Ontario. He is the author of many volumes of poetry and several memoirs.

Slouching Toward Tomorrow

Sometimes we feel like
          orphans of light, powerless be-
fore the jagged debris of
          a broken world. Sometimes we
stand at a crossroads under
          a darkening sky that no longer
whispers of infinite stars,
          baffled how we became so lost,
whether we will ever recover
          those crude maps of thinking
locked with all our good
          intentions in caves of memor-
abilia. But just when all
          seems black, our path in doubt,
nothing between us & the
          latched windows of heaven, an
inner voice impels us to
          question the brute force of dark-
ness, search again for that
          one small curl of redeeming fire—
the herald of a new tomorrow.

Night Songs

Melinda Burns

Melinda Burns is a writer and a psychotherapist in private practice in Guelph, Ontario, where she also teaches writing. Her writing has won awards for fiction, including first prize in the Toronto Star Short Story contest in 2001 and first prize in the Elora Writers' Festival Writing Contest in 2008. She has published poems in various magazines, read her essays on CBC radio, and published essays on writing in Canadian Notes and Queries and in K.D. Miller's book on creativity and spirituality, Holy Writ. *Melinda lives in Guelph.*

Night Songs

She's recording birds' night songs
outside her third floor room
trying to figure out what they are

She sends them to me
thinking her mom might know
I don't but I listen

to their heartfelt notes pouring
out in the darkness
while we are all confined

in a pandemic night
I open my windows
to drink it in

A Song in That

Rob O'Flanagan

Rob O'Flanagan has been a newspaper reporter, photojournalist and columnist for nearly twenty years. He has won numerous Ontario Newspaper Awards and a National Newspaper Award. He is the author of The Stories We Tell *and* The Blown Kiss Collection, *two volumes of short fiction, and* Open Up the Sky: A Poetic Conversation, *co-authored with Heather Cardin. He writes, performs and records poetry, and is a visual artist.*

A Song in That

Wish I could play
that wind on my
guitar
      Then I'd sing
      something to it
      about light feet
      and laying down to
      rest

The bucket tilts on the
truck and spills a sweetness
into the muddy field
      I wish I could play
      that on my harmonica

Friends should come over
and play to my words

There's a song in this
I could sing

afterimage

Sheri Doyle

Sheri Doyle is an editor and author who works with educational publishers, trade publishers, and individual authors. She also writes poetry and fiction.

afterimage

baby kangaroo, newly out
of your mother's fleshy pouch,
we can be more than
the horrified spectators
of a viral photograph–
our thumbs hovering over
your limbs clenched to a wire fence

we can do more than
pause in our scroll and dream
of guiding you into a field of grass
  or the softness of shadows where
   ferns and mosses are heavy with dew
of leading you back to your mother

was that her in The New York Times
dashing before a burning house
across our orange lit phones–
her silhouette is the afterimage
on our white walls when we look up
in our dining rooms, spotted
on the mirrors of our bathrooms
or in our bedrooms on the windowpanes
  she is springing through glass
  onto clouds parting in twilight
  and now in the opening where
  on the full moon rising
  she leaps from flames in search of you

the early bird

Sheila Koop

Sheila Koop writes poetry, short stories, bits of creative nonfiction and is currently working on a novel for preteens. Her poem "Purple Voyage" won first prize at the 2003 Elora Writer's Festival Competition, and her short story, "The Arcana of Living Springs", was awarded Honourable Mention for the 2014 Elora Writers Festival competition.

the early bird

the earliest bird is up
before the sun takes her place
jittery stars have faded out
now the uninterrupted sunlight
appears in patches on the fence
hydrangea and cucumber vines crowd
together with blossom and fruit
we take coffee and check the weather
the tomato plants seem exhausted
flutter of shadow breezes through the tall maples

life distilled in a quiet morning

Rejection Letter

Tom Vaine

Tom Vaine lives in Elora, Ontario, and works as a high school teacher. He has a graduate degree in Literature Studies, with a focus on speculative fiction. Tom's stories have appeared in Bewildering Stories *online magazine as well as* Rhapsody, Guelph's *annual poetry collection.*

Rejection Letter

Their letter said, "we won't be able", as
though the things I wrote might tear the page and run
amok despite them, or perhaps they felt
their passions running wild as the read and so
they had to keep it for themselves.
I think I like that second notion best.

 But the truth is I'm a sock drawer poet
of worn rhymes and frayed clichés,
a scrap-knee poet
of bent spokes and unoiled chains,
gap-tooth poet
of overalls and deep grass stains,
a beer-mouth poet
of mumbled voice and garbled phrase.

 As such my words may prove too rough,
too rude, too boisterous for some to hear,
but let them turn away. At least they won't
be able to claim I have nothing to say.

Vocamus Writers Community

Vocamus Writers Community is a non-profit community organization that supports book culture in Guelph and the surrounding area. It runs workshops, writing groups, and writer hang-outs. It offers resources for writers looking to publish their work both traditionally and independently. It promotes readings, launches, and other literary events in the community. It also produces the annual *Rhapsody* anthology Guelph area poetry. For more information, email vocamuswriterscommunity@gmail.com.

www.ingramcontent.com/pod-product-compliance
Lightning Source LLC
Chambersburg PA
CBHW031216090426
42736CB00009B/942